SURVIVAL AND LOSS
Native American Boarding Schools

Developmental Studies Center • Oakland, California

First edition published 2008.

Photographs, maps, paintings, and images: *The Native American Experience* by Carter Smith, executive editor. Copyright © 1991 published by Facts On File, an imprint of Infobase Publishing (pp. 3, 5, 6, 13, 24, 25); National Park Service, www.nps.gov (p. 4); wyomingtalesandtrails.com courtesy Wyoming Tales and Trails (p. 7); Getty Images, Inc. Copyright © 1999–2008 Getty Images, Inc. All rights reserved. (p. 11); Denver Public Library (p. 15, cover); National Archives, American Indian Select List number 152 (p. 19); Library of Congress, www.loc.gov (pp. 20, 23, 26).

Illustrations: Marjorie C. Leggitt (pp. 8–9, 10–11, 12–13, 14–15, 16–17)

Cover and interior designs: Karen McClinchey

Developmental Studies Center
2000 Embarcadero, Suite 305
Oakland, CA 94606-5300
(800) 666-7270, fax: (510) 464-3670
www.devstu.org

ISBN-13: 978-1-59892-746-7
ISBN-10: 1-59892-746-9

Printed in Mexico
 2 3 4 5 6 7 8 9 10 RRD 17 16 15 14 13 12 11 10 09

— CONTENTS —

In the eyes of Native American people, children have a special purpose. They are given to Earth by the spirit world to bring new life and strength to the world of the living. When European people began to arrive in North America in 1492, passing on Native American beliefs like these became a great struggle.

The travelers from Europe believed that their way of life was more advanced than Native Americans'. They studied at schools and universities, while the Native Americans had no written language and learned by hearing stories told aloud. Native Americans used tools made from animal bones and fish lures fashioned from shells. The Europeans had metal tools and weapons, giving them a powerful advantage over the Native American people. Because of differences such as these, most Europeans decided that Native Americans were savages—people who had never learned the ways of **civilization**.

When the United States was formed in 1776, Native Americans were not included as citizens. All of their rights, including their rights to the land they had lived on for thousands of years, were ignored. The U.S. government fought Native American tribes for their land and won every time, but the government was then faced with the issue of what place Native Americans had in this new country. They called this "the Indian problem."

To deal with the "problem," the U.S. government decided to give Native American children a European-style education. The children were taken away from their families and the lives they knew and sent to boarding schools. There, it was hoped, they would learn to live like other American citizens. This book tells their story.

Naming the Native Peoples

The explorer Christopher Columbus gave the native peoples of America the name *Indians*. In fact, the native peoples of the Americas had no name for themselves as a whole. They called one another by the names of their tribes, or groups.

The name of each tribe reflected its certain way of life. For example, one tribe called itself Arapaho, which comes from a word that means "traders."

However, the differences between tribes were not clear to Europeans. It was easier for them to apply one name to all of the native peoples than to learn to recognize each tribe.

Today, many terms are used to describe the native peoples of America. In this book, we use the term Native Americans.

1. Broken Promises

THE TRAIL OF TEARS

I n the 1800s, European settlers flooded into the United States. As they began building new lives for themselves—mining for gold and building towns, farms, canals, and railroads—they took over more and more land.

In 1836, the U.S. government tried to resolve its "Indian problem" by giving the eastern Native American tribes two years to move westward from their homelands. If these tribes didn't move within the two-year period, they would be forced to leave. While many tribes had little choice but to go, some tribes fought against removal.

For example, only 2,000 of the 18,000 Native Americans in the area known today as Georgia had moved by the end of the two years. In 1838, government soldiers force-marched the Cherokee and other tribes from Georgia all the

Painting by Robert Lindneux, Woolaroc Museum, Bartlesville, Oklahoma

"It is with sorrow we are forced by the white man to quit the scenes of our childhood. We bid farewell to it and all we hold dear."

—Charles Hicks, Cherokee chief

3

1. Broken Promises

way to present-day Oklahoma. During the long, difficult journey of more than 1,000 miles, about 4,000 people became ill and died. This journey became known as the Trail of Tears.

Present-day Oklahoma was set aside as Native American territory. However, this land was different from the land the eastern tribes were used to. The crops they had grown in the East didn't grow on the new land, there were few wild animals to hunt, and the plants and geography were unfamiliar. The Native Americans had no way to rebuild the life they had built for themselves in the East. Even as the tribes struggled to survive in Oklahoma, much of the land they had been given was taken back by the U.S. government as the population of white settlers grew.

THE RESERVATIONS

The plains (or western) tribes were also struggling to survive. When gold was discovered in California in 1849, a flood of white settlers began traveling west hoping to make their fortunes, passing through Native American hunting grounds on the way. Tensions began to build as the two peoples crossed paths.

Unlike Native Americans, the settlers were not respectful of the land. They cut down many trees and hunted too many animals. There were so many violent **confrontations** between Native Americans and settlers that the U.S. government became worried that there might be a full-scale war.

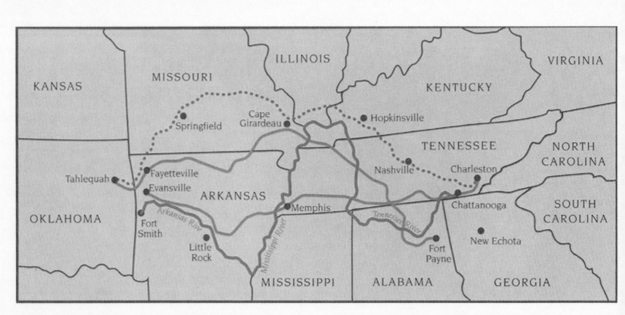

Cherokee Removal Routes This map shows four different Cherokee removal routes. Most of the tribes walked from Georgia to Oklahoma. Some traveled by a combination of wagon, boat, and horse.

Native Americans fought hard to combat the sudden flood of settlers into their homelands.

In 1851, in an attempt to keep the Native Americans out of the settlers' way, the U.S. Congress introduced the Indian **Appropriation** Act. The act said the Lakota, Cheyenne, Arapaho, Crow, and other western tribes would live on areas of land known as reservations until they stopped attacking the settlers. Each tribe was given a specific piece of land. The U.S. government agreed that the tribes would receive a yearly payment for as long as they lived on the reservations, but soon the U.S. government reduced the number of years for payment. In some cases, the U.S. government had promised the same land to more than one tribe, and fights broke out between the tribes as they competed for water, game, and land. As more and more settlers moved westward in search of gold and land, the government also made the reservations smaller.

Lost Land, Lost Independence

COAST TO COAST

With the building of the **first transcontinental railroad**, a continuous train track running all the way from the east coast to the west coast of the U.S., Native Americans lost even more territory. Railroad companies needed land to build tracks. And when the transcontinental railroad was completed in 1869, the cross-country trains made it much easier for settlers to move west. Railroad companies encouraged people to build towns near the tracks because bigger settlements meant more train passengers. But to the Native Americans, more settlers meant less land.

CHIEF RED CLOUD AND THE TREATY OF FORT LARAMIE

At the same time the transcontinental railroad was nearing completion, the U.S. government signed the Treaty of Fort Laramie to stop the Sioux, led by the great chief Red Cloud, from attacking settlers and raiding U.S. government forts. The treaty promised to extend a Sioux reservation to include the Black Hills of South Dakota, the most sacred lands of the Sioux. However, when gold was found in the Black Hills, the U.S. government replaced the treaty with a new agreement taking back the land.

Painting by N.H. Trotter. Smithsonian Institution.

Trains were a threat to herds of bison. These large, ox-like animals were an important resource for the Native Americans.

To sign the Indian Appropriation Act, more than 10,000 Native Americans gathered near Fort Laramie, Wyoming. Not knowing how to read or write, their leaders signed the agreement by touching the pen.

When Red Cloud traveled to Washington, D.C., to protest the broken treaty, he was told by government officials that he had signed a treaty giving away the tribe's land rather than protecting it. "We could not read the treaty," Red Cloud responded. "We did not know what it said."

After seeing the large cities that white Americans had built in the East, Red Cloud realized that Native Americans could never win a full-scale war against the settlers. One by one, the proud warrior chiefs admitted defeat and were forced onto smaller reservations.

"We could not read the treaty.
We did not know what it said."

—Red Cloud, chief of the Sioux tribe

Lost Land, Lost Independence

WARDS OF THE STATE

In 1871, all Native American tribes lost their right to sign treaties when the U.S. government declared that it no longer recognized the tribes as nations, but instead thought of Native Americans as "wards of the state." A ward of the state is a person who cannot take responsibility for himself or herself, such as a young child.

U.S. troops and government agents took control of the reservations. The agents distributed rations of food and secondhand clothes. The Native Americans were treated as if they could not care for themselves, and on the reservations, this became true. The Native Americans were forced to depend on the government because they no longer had the resources they needed to make a living. They were a long way from the land they knew.

The reservations were on land that none of the settlers wanted. Many of the tribes had never learned to farm in the European American way, and the poor-quality soil on the reservations made it impossible to learn. So many bison had been killed to make way for the building of the railroad that there were not enough bison to hunt. The tribes could not feed themselves or their families.

Now the United States had a different kind of "Indian problem." Native Americans were no longer **self-sufficient**. If they were not able to provide for themselves on the reservations, their children would not learn how to provide for themselves, either.

Marjorie C. Leggitt

3. Life on the Reservations

LOST TRADITIONS

Native Americans felt a **sacred** connection to the land. Their whole way of life was bound to where they lived. When Native Americans were forced to move from their land to the reservations, each tribe left behind the special way of life it had known.

The Cherokee people, for example, before they were moved to the dry, grassy area that is now Oklahoma, lived in forests along riverbanks. Families lived in lodges in small villages. The men hunted deer, turtles, and bears and carved wood into canoes. Women wove baskets from river reeds and made clothes from animal skins. They planted beans, corn, and squash, surrounding them with tobacco plants, which were used as medicine. The Cherokee people believed that they should respect plants and animals. They appreciated what nature gave them and never took more than they needed. Cherokee people tried to keep a balance in their world.

Several times each year, villages showed their respect for the land by holding ceremonies. One kind of ceremony celebrated the harvesting of crops. The people would **fast** and clean their lodges, and then hold an all-day feast, followed by dancing, singing, and games.

These kinds of ceremonies didn't make sense on the reservations. Native Americans living on reservations were given foods such as fatback (fat from a pig's back), hardtack (hard biscuits made from flour and water), and coffee to drink. The once-proud tribes now depended on the U.S. government to live. When food was scarce, they begged for food from soldiers.

"For each tribe of men God created, he also made a home. In the land for any particular tribe, God also placed whatever would be best for that tribe."

—Geronimo, chief of the Apache tribe of the southwestern United States

PUSHED TOWARD THE CLASSROOM

Native American children did not go to school; instead, they learned by watching adults. They helped their parents at work and learned skills by playing games such as lacrosse, a sport similar to soccer played with sticks and a ball. At night, when families shared meals around a fire, the children heard stories about great leaders and myths about animals and nature that helped them understand the reasons behind their tribe's way of life.

The U.S. government believed that Native American children needed a more formal education in order to fit into the European American world. It built schools on the reservations to teach the children English and skills such as carpentry, but attendance at the schools was poor. Children would often run away from their classrooms. Or, if they heard the sound of tribal drums, rush to join their families. Many parents refused to let their children attend classes.

"Almost every evening, a myth or a true story of some deed done in the past was narrated by one of the parents or grandparents while the boy listened with parted lips and glistening eyes."

—Charles A. Eastman of the Sioux tribe

Marjorie C. Leggitt

THE BOARDING SCHOOL SOLUTION

Some government officials, especially one man named Captain Richard Henry Pratt, believed that the best way to **Americanize** Native American children was to educate them in boarding schools, away from their families and tribes. Captain Pratt believed that Native Americans should be forced to live in the English-speaking world and that it was necessary to "kill the Indian to save the man." In other words, he believed that Native Americans should be taken away from their traditions so that they had no choice but to learn the ways of European Americans.

In 1879, the U.S. government gave Captain Pratt an old army fort in Carlisle, Pennsylvania, so that he could build a boarding school. Pratt modeled the new school, named the Carlisle Indian Industrial School, on schools for prisoners.

Pratt had to persuade Native American chiefs to send their children to the school. At first, the chiefs refused. Spotted Tail, a Sioux chief, said, "The white man knew there was gold in the Black Hills, and he made us agree to give up all that country. We do not want our children to learn such things."

"You cannot read or write," Pratt responded. "Because you were not educated, these mountains, valleys, and streams have passed from you."* Pratt argued that if Native Americans could speak the English language, they would not be defenseless. Reluctantly, Spotted Tail agreed to send the children of the Sioux tribe to the school.

Photograph, Smithsonian Institute National Anthropological Archives

Spotted Tail and his wife (pictured) finally sent their children to Carlisle Indian Industrial School.

"Because you were not educated, these mountains, valleys, and streams have passed from you."

—Captain Richard Henry Pratt

*Quote from Michael L. Cooper's Indian School (Clarion Books: New York, 1999)

Marjorie C. Leggitt

Boarding School Life

THE JOURNEY

In October 1879, 82 boys and girls began their journey from South Dakota to Carlisle Indian Industrial School. When they boarded the train, they were told that they were "going to school." They didn't know why they were taken from their homes, how far they would travel, or whether they would see their families again. One boy, named Ota Kte, thought that they were going to be killed. However, believing that he was doing something brave for his tribe, Ota Kte boarded the train with the others.

The long, noisy train ride was the first of many strange experiences for the children. Whenever the train stopped in a city, crowds of people stared at them, curious to see the "wild" children. The children huddled inside, frightened and confused.

"BEFORE" AND "AFTER"

When the hungry, exhausted children arrived at Carlisle, Captain Pratt's program began immediately. First, the children were photographed. Next, they were stripped of their traditional clothing, including the special beaded necklaces their parents had given them to mark an important journey or change in their lives. Everything was placed in a pile and burned. The children were then scrubbed in hot baths and given uniforms to wear. The children were used to wearing loose clothing and soft moccasins on their feet, so the stiff collars, belts, and boots made them feel trapped and **anxious**. They felt as if they were locked in cages.

Captain Pratt also thought that the boys' long hair made them look like savages and had it cut short. Traditionally, the only time Native Americans cut their hair was during times of **mourning**. The children wailed as it was cut.

Finally, with their new clothes and short hair, the children were photographed again.

NEW NAMES

At the school, the children were **immersed** in English. Immersion is a way of teaching foreign languages in which teachers and students use only the foreign language. The children were forbidden to speak their native languages at any time. They had no way to express their feelings of homesickness and confusion because they didn't know the English words for their thoughts and feelings. If Native American

Marjorie C. Leggitt

Pratt wanted to show "before" and "after" photographs to people so that he could prove that he had "civilized" the children.

What's in a Name?

Native American names are given to honor what a person has done or what qualities he or she has. For example, the Cherokee name *Ayita* means "first to dance" and the Sioux name *Hantaywee* means "faithful." *Ota Kte*, meaning "plenty kill," had been given his name to honor his father's skills as a warrior.

children spoke their native languages at school, they were made to wash their own mouths with soap.

As part of their English language immersion, the children chose English names for themselves from a list on a chalkboard. The names belonged to U.S. presidents and other important people, but the scribbles on the chalkboard meant nothing to the children. With new names and appearances, the children no longer felt like themselves.

UNFAMILIAR ROUTINES

At mealtimes, the children had to march like soldiers to long dining tables. They waited for a bell to ring before sitting down to eat. The children had never sat at tables or used knives, forks, and napkins before. Most had never eaten such foods as flour or sugar.

The children became sick because of their new diet and because they were living in such close quarters. Diseases then spread quickly in the crowded, drafty **dormitories**. The children had no **immunity** against illnesses such as measles, mumps, and influenza. In the first year, 6 boys died and 15 children were sent home ill.

As bad as the days were, the nights were worse. As one Sioux woman, Zitkala-Sa, later wrote, "Not a soul came to comfort me. I was only one of many little animals driven by a herder." The dormitories were very strange to the children. At home, there was no furniture, and families slept together in round **tepees** and lodges, but at Carlisle, beds were arranged in long rows, and the children were forbidden to speak to one another.

Marjorie C. Leggitt

RUNAWAYS

At Carlisle and other Native American boarding schools, homesick children tried to run away— even if they were thousands of miles from home. Sometimes parents of runaways were able to help their children get home, but more often, runaways were caught and punished harshly as an example to their fellow students. A student might be beaten with a strap or locked in a room for hours.

Some parents refused to let their children be taken to boarding schools, but families who resisted were denied food rations or threatened by U.S. police or soldiers. Parents hid their children or sent them running, but the children were almost always chased and caught or frightened out of hiding. Their arms and legs were tied, and they were tossed into wagons and taken to school.

KEEPING CULTURE ALIVE

The students found small ways to rebel against boarding school life. Many refused to respond to their teachers. If a teacher asked a question, a student might stare into space, blank faced and silent. Some students would deliberately do their work very slowly. As a result, many teachers believed that the children were unintelligent.

Outside the classroom, the students were not silent. They would give teachers nicknames in their native languages. One teacher, for example, was given the nickname "Woman Who Makes You Scream." The students also re-created Native American ceremonies.

At night, they lit candles and told stories. In the fields outside the school, they built fires and roasted corn. They made tiny **tom-toms** out of tin cans and danced. Even though their culture was forbidden, the students tried to keep it alive.

5. Lessons and Learning

ENTERING A STRANGE WORLD

Being immersed in English was a big challenge for Native American children. Because teachers didn't know Native American languages, they couldn't translate words for students. Instead they labeled objects, such as "desk," "chair," and "book." However, most Native Americans had never used written language. So the idea that words could be written down with symbols on paper was completely new to the children.

Also, learning English meant learning to express ideas differently. For example, a Native American verb for "rain" might give extra information about the rain, such as how a rainstorm happened, where it rained, or how much it rained. English verbs for "rain" told only if it had rained or if it was still raining. To speak English, Native American children had to learn to think in a new way.

Learning about time was also a challenge. Native Americans had learned to live by natural measurements of time, not by a clock. At school, the children were on a strict schedule. Bells rang to tell them when to get up, to eat, to go to class, and to sleep.

When the students could speak a little English, they were taught subjects such as science and history. Often, these lessons didn't fit with Native American beliefs. In science lessons, for example, students were shocked to be told that the Earth was not flat and that stars were bigger than Earth. In lessons on American history, the students were told that settlers had defeated Native Americans for their own good. They were also taught that they should be grateful to European Americans for bringing "civilization" to their world.

Because the Native American children were being prepared for a life of hard work, subjects such as music and art were considered a waste of time for them. Instead, the students were made to do most of the work of cleaning and maintaining the schools and were often left too tired to study at all.

Sioux boys as they were dressed on arrival at the Carlisle Indian Industrial School. Photographed by J. N. Choate, October 5, 1879.

"Hours, minutes, and seconds were such small divisions of time that we had never thought of them. When we went on a hunting trip or to a sun dance, we counted time by sleeps."

—Carl Sweezy, Arapaho tribe

NEW SKILLS

Adapting to the "civilized" American way of life meant learning new skills. This, the U.S. government thought, was the only way that Native American children would survive in this new and unfamiliar world. They had been taught jobs such as housekeeping and carpentry at schools on the reservations, but the boarding schools taught other skills as well.

Because the government believed that Native Americans could earn a living as farmers, farming was the primary skill taught at the

Pupils at Carlisle Indian Industrial School, 1900

boarding schools. Planting crops and raising animals also provided food for the teachers and students. While the boys farmed, the girls did domestic work such as cleaning and sewing.

Native American children also learned about a **cash economy**. At Carlisle, for example, the students earned a little money for their work, which they put into savings accounts. If students were chosen to join a special program called the Outing Program, they could save more.

The Outing Program

In the Outing Program, a student would leave school during the summer months to live with a white family and go to work. The students had to follow rules, such as saving a regular amount of money. The most important rule was to obey their employers.

The program worked well at Carlisle, where most neighboring families tried to help the Native American children fit in. Many students learned more skills here, such as gardening and cooking. However, the program failed at other boarding schools. People in the West were more prejudiced toward Native Americans. They said that the students were unwilling to work, and they often treated them cruelly. These students felt alone and unhappy.

6. Boarding Schools in Question

A GOOD INVESTMENT?

The Carlisle school opened in 1879. Initially, the U.S. government saw Carlisle as a great success. Other boarding schools for Native American children began to open. By 1902, there were 25 boarding schools in 15 states, and very few Native American students were left attending day schools on the reservations. Almost 10,000 children were enrolled in boarding schools.

However, despite the $45 million spent between 1880 and 1900 to "educate" about 20,000 Native American children in the ways of European American society, very few students actually graduated from the schools. For example, only 8 percent of the students who attended Carlisle ever graduated. Many students ran away, and many of those who remained were not educated—or Americanized—in the way supporters of the schools had hoped. Some people in the U.S. government began to question how well the schools really worked.

THE MERIAM REPORT

In 1928, the U.S. government could see that many of its Native American policies had failed. A researcher named Lewis Meriam was sent to prepare a report about the conditions on Native American reservations and in boarding schools. Meriam led a team of experts, including scientists, historians, teachers, and lawyers. They found that in all areas of life, Native Americans were suffering—especially children in boarding schools. Just a few of the findings in Meriam's report, called "The Problem of Indian Administration," were:

- Health conditions in boarding schools were terrible.

- A diet lacking in nutrients was causing children to become ill.

- Schools considered work such as farming and cleaning to be more important than classroom education.

- Schools followed **rigid** routines that stopped children from being creative.

- Lessons should include Native American subjects to help students feel more comfortable in unfamiliar classrooms.

CLOSED FOR GOOD

At the time of the Meriam Report, almost 80 percent of Native American school-aged children were in boarding schools. The report was embarrassing for the U.S. government because it showed that children should not be taken away from their homes to be educated.

The strict routines and teaching style of boarding schools had done little to help Native American students learn. This photograph shows students during a mathematics class at Carlisle.

Meriam and his team concluded that Native American children should instead attend day schools or public schools that would keep them connected to their families and communities. By the 1930s, most of the boarding schools, including Carlisle, had been closed for good.

Long-term Effects

EFFECTS ON THE STUDENTS

The schools' drastic efforts to **suppress** Native American ways damaged many children forever. "When we enter the school, we at least know that we are Indians," said John Fire, writing about his experience at a boarding school. "We come out half-red and half-white, not knowing what we are."

The schools had taken away much of what the Native Americans knew but had failed to provide them with knowledge that they could easily use to improve their lives or the lives of their tribes. As Lewis Meriam wrote in his report, students had learned skills such as "printing, when the Indians rarely read and have no paper; shoemaking, when most of them wear moccasins made by the women; painting, when the houses are made of logs." If Native American children left their reservations to search for jobs, they faced **prejudice** and were unable to compete with white people for work.

Even if Native Americans rejected what they had learned at school, it was difficult to return to their old way of life. They were trapped between two worlds: They no longer felt a part of the tribes they had left behind, and they knew they did not belong in the world outside the reservations, either.

Some students had lost the ability to communicate altogether. Immersion had kept them from speaking their native language but had not taught them English. They suffered in silence.

1775

■ Native American land claimed by European settlers
□ Land held by Native Americans

EFFECTS ON NATIVE AMERICAN CULTURE AS A WHOLE

For most Native American children, the boarding schools caused a loss of cultural identity. In other words, the children lost the knowledge of how their tribes lived because they didn't have the experience of living and working in their families and communities. They lost the traditions and beliefs they would have learned through tribal ceremonies and stories. Native American children who went to the boarding schools were unable to continue their tribes' ways of life.

The Native Americans had suffered from war and diseases. They had lost almost all their land. They were humiliated on the reservations because they were unable to take care of themselves. The final blow was the most painful: They had lost their children. The effects of this suffering are still felt in the lives of Native Americans today.

1894

■ Native American land claimed by European settlers
■ Land held by Native Americans

Over the years, Native Americans were forced onto smaller and smaller parcels of land. Without large pieces of land, they could not continue their way of life.

HOPE FOR THE FUTURE

Young Native Americans who attended boarding schools lost their sense of who they were. In return, they gained only knowledge of a world that continued to exclude them. Yet a few Native Americans found ways to use their new knowledge. Little by little, they worked for the rights of all Native Americans. They knew enough about the European American world to be able to reason with the government and to inform all Americans about the damage that had been done to Native American culture. It was the first step in bringing to light centuries of injustice and the first step toward healing the wounds.

Zitkala-Sa wrote many stories and articles about her experience at Carlisle Indian Industrial School (see Appendix A for an example). She and others worked hard for Native American rights. Because of these efforts, the U.S. government passed the Indian Citizenship Act of 1924.

Luther Standing Bear

The boy named Ota Kte became Luther Standing Bear—a writer, actor, and teacher. In the 1920s and 30s, he fought to improve conditions for people who lived on the reservations. He wrote about his feelings in his book *My Indian Boyhood*: "If today I had a young mind to direct, to start on the journey of life, and I was faced with the duty of choosing between the natural way of my forefathers and that of the present way of civilization, I would set that child's feet in the path of my forefathers. I would raise him to be an Indian!"

— APPENDIX A —
THE WORD "NO"

A short time after our arrival, we three Dakotas were playing in the snowdrifts. We were all still deaf to the English language, excepting Judewin. One morning, we learned through her ears that we were forbidden to fall in the snow. However, before many hours, we were having great sport in the snow, when a shrill voice called us.

Judewin said: "Now the pale face is going to punish us for falling into the snow. If she talks loudly, you must wait until she stops. Then, after a tiny pause, say, 'No.'"

The rest of the way we practiced the little word "no."

As it happened, Thowin was summoned first. The door shut behind her with a click.

Judewin and I stood silently listening at the keyhole. Judewin heard enough of the words to realize all too late that she had taught us the wrong reply.

"Oh, poor Thowin!" she gasped as she put both hands over her ears.

Just then I heard Thowin's tremulous answer, "No."

With an angry exclamation, the woman gave her a hard spanking. Then she stopped to say something. Judewin said it was this: "Are you going to obey my word the next time?"

Thowin answered again with the only word at her command, "No."

Zitkala-Sa (1985). American Indian Stories. *Lincoln: University of Nebraska Press.*

— APPENDIX B —
MAJOR EVENTS IN NATIVE AMERICAN HISTORY

1492   North America becomes known to Europeans.

1776   United States becomes a nation.

1838–1839   Trail of Tears takes place.

1849   California Gold Rush begins.

1851   Indian Appropriation Act is passed.

1861   American Civil War begins.

1865   American Civil War ends.

1869   First transcontinental railroad is completed.

1871   Tribes are deprived of separate-nation status.

1876   Black Hills gold miners invade Sioux lands.

1879   Carlisle Indian Industrial School is founded by Captain Pratt.

1918   Carlisle Indian Industrial School is closed.

1928   Meriam Report condemns boarding schools.

— GLOSSARY —

Americanize: to make someone adopt an American way of life

anxious: worried and uneasy

appropriation: using something without permission

cash economy: a system of buying and selling goods that uses money

civilization: a society that has many social, political, and cultural systems (Though Native Americans had their own civilization, the settlers did not recognize it. They believed that European civilization was the only real one.)

confrontation: a face-to-face meeting

dormitory: a large bedroom for a number of people

fast: to go without eating for a period of time

first transcontinental railroad: a railroad built across North America in the 1860s, linking the eastern United States to California in the West, completed in Utah on May 10, 1869

immersed: completely involved in an activity

immunity: natural protection against diseases

mourning: expressing deep sorrow, as for someone who has died

prejudice: belief that one group of people is inferior to another, based on lack of knowledge or understanding about that group

rigid: strict and unchanging

sacred: worthy of special respect and worship

self-sufficient: able to provide what is needed, such as food and shelter, without help from others

suppress: to hold back

tepee: a cone-shaped tent made from animal skins and branches or wooden poles

tom-toms: small, narrow hand drums

— INDEX —